I
love
myself

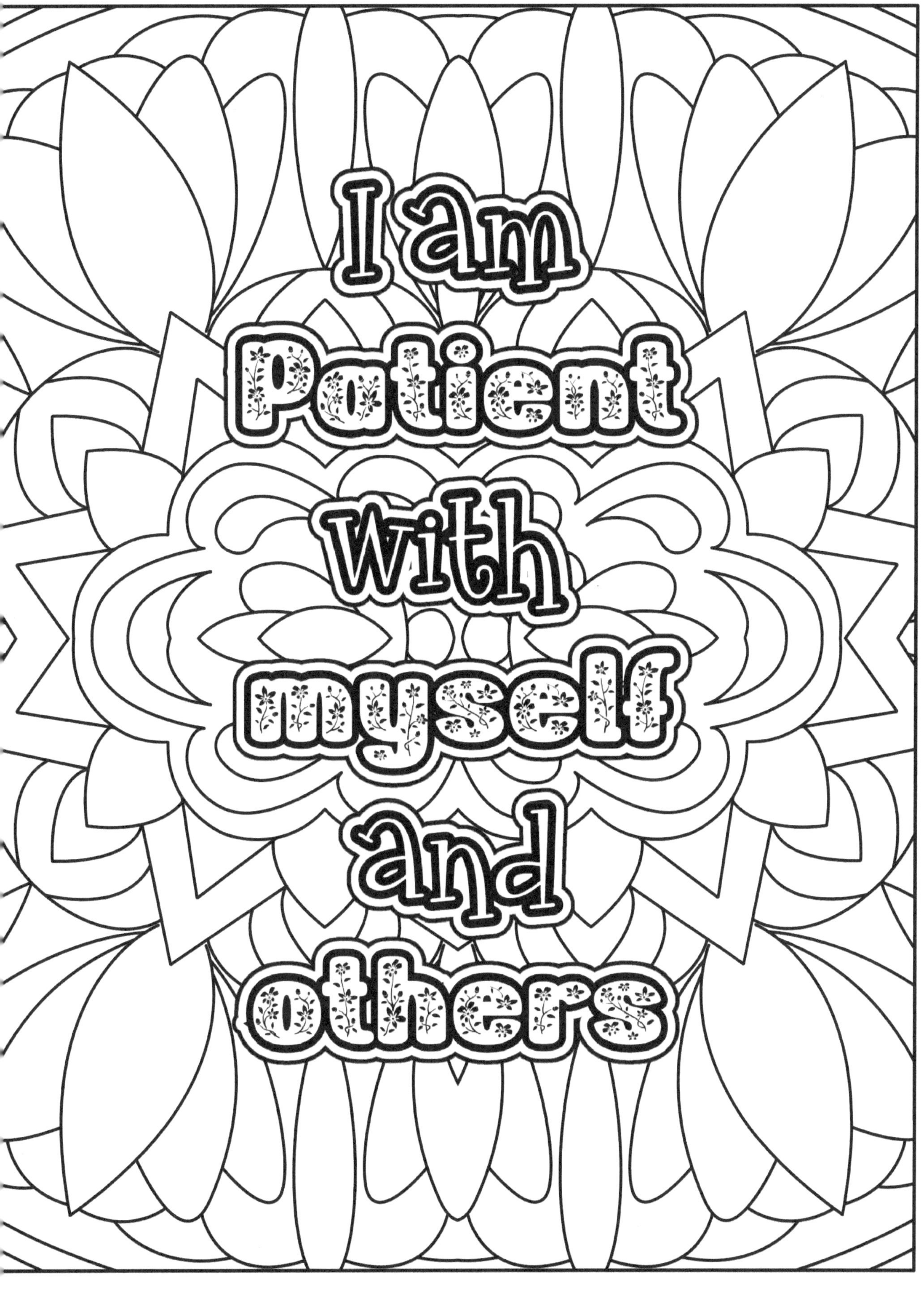
I am
Patient
With
myself
and
others

I speak with
KINDNESS

I am
BRAVE
enough
to TRY

I CARE
ABOUT
OTHERS

I CAN
TRY
AGAIN

I matter

I PRACTICE
to improve

I STRIVE
to do
MY BEST

I AM
ENOUGH

mistakes
are
how
we
GROW

I talk about my
FEELINGS

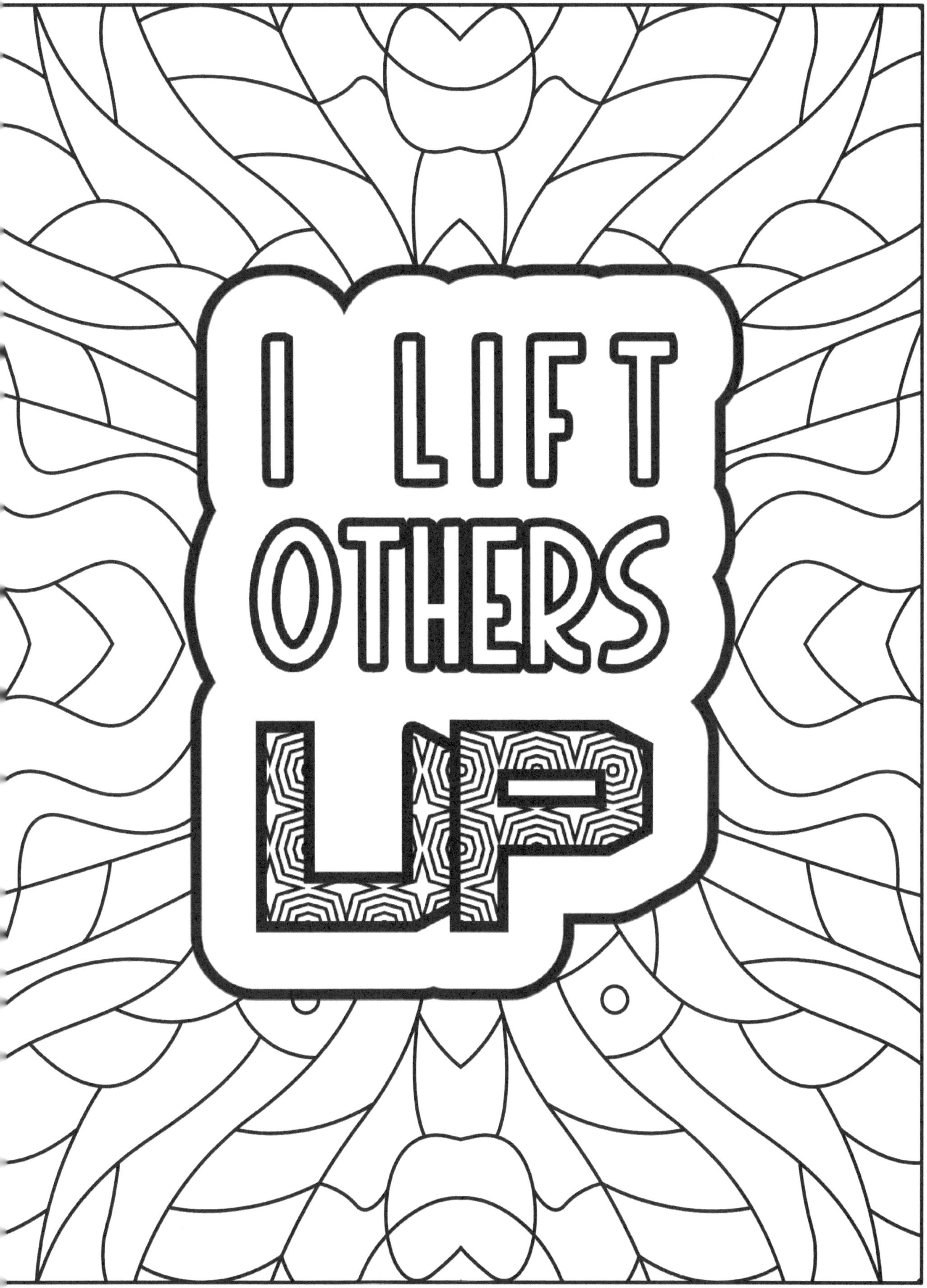
I LIFT
OTHERS
UP

I FORGiVE
OTHERS
FOR THEiR
mistakes

I deserve
HAPPINESS

I CAN
make
GOOD
choices

I HAVE
A KIND
Heart

I AM IN
CONTROL
OF MY
ACTIONS

EVEN
WHEN I
STRUGGLE
I KEEP GOING

I CAN DO
HARD
THINGS

I CHOOSE
TO HAVE
POSITIVE
THOUGHTS

I choose MY attitude

I
AM
STRONG

MY WORDS
HAVE
POWER

I WiLL NOT
COMPARE
MYSELF
TO OTHERS

Made in United States
Troutdale, OR
05/25/2024

20103029R00031